Online Business

Simple Yet Effective Ideas on How To Make Money Online And Generate High Amounts Of Passive Income

Anthony Parker

Copyright © 2017 Anthony Parker

All rights reserved.

It is not legal to reproduce, duplicate, or transmit any part of this document by either electronic means or printed format. Recording of this publication is strictly prohibited

ISBN:1979001634
ISBN-13:9781979001632

TABLE OF CONTENTS

Introduction i

Chapter One: Everything You Should Know About Dropshipping 1

Chapter Two: How To Use Shopify For Dropshipping ... 15

Chapter Three: How To Make A Business With Kindle Publishing 21

Chapter Four: Finding Freelance Work 29

Chapter Five: Making Online Courses 42

Chapter Six: Making Money With Cryptocurrency Trading And Investing 50

Chapter Seven: How To Make Money Blogging 58

Chapter Eight: Making Money Through Affiliate Marketing 63

Final Words 68

About the author 69

Introduction

Thank you for taking the time to purchase this book: *Online Business: Simple yet Effective Ideas on How To Make Money Online and Generate High Amounts of Passive Income.* You have just taken the first step towards setting up your own online business and discovering ways of making money online, both actively and passively.

This book covers the topic of starting your own online business and becoming your own boss. It will teach you everything you need to know about dropshipping, Kindle Publishing, freelancing, creating online courses, trading and investing in cryptocurrency, blogging, and affiliate marketing. You will learn ways of earning a passive income online and making a living as a freelancer.

At the completion of this book, you will have a good understanding of how to make money with an online business. Many people make thousands of dollars per month online, and this book will show you how that is possible. You will also be able to define the area you want to work in and identify your audience. This will help you create a product or service that is specially tailored for a tight, loyal target market and enjoy a profitable relationship with your clients in exchange for the value you provide.

Once again, thanks for purchasing this book, I hope you find it to be helpful!.

Chapter One: Everything You Should Know About Dropshipping

In this chapter, we will look at something called dropshipping and see how it can be used to create a profitable online business.

First of all, what is dropshipping?

Dropshipping is a type of supply chain process. The merchant or online store that uses the dropshipping method doesn't keep the product it sells in stock. Instead, every time the merchant sells a product, it will purchase that specific product from a supplier who will also ship the product to the customer. This way, the merchant never sees the product, handles the product, or ships the product. This is all left to the supplier.

This process contrasts with the standard retail model where a merchant would either design and create their own products to sell or buy in bulk from a manufacturer to then send directly to the customer as they buy from the store. The standard retail model makes the merchant responsible for more parts of the supply chain. The dropshipping model, however, frees the store – known as a dropshipper - from having the responsibility of holding onto inventory or shipping the products, placing that instead in the hands of the manufacturer. The dropshippers still set their own product prices, considering the cost of the wholesale product, fees, and desired profit margin. A profit margin is the difference between what the dropshipper pays the supplier and what they charge the customer.

The main advantage of doing this is that it takes out the stress and cost of buying in bulk and sending out products. It also opens the doors to those wanting to set up an online business with ease. It depends on working with a wholesaler or distributor that works in the dropshipping business. It is important to establish an excellent partnership to facilitate communication about shipping times and stock levels.

To sum up, there are three necessary steps to dropshipping:

> ➢ The customer makes a purchase which generates an order on the dropshipper's (merchant or online store) site.
>
> ➢ The drop shipper then makes the same order with their supplier.
> ➢ The supplier receives the order and then sends the product directly to the customer who placed the order.

How Can You Make Money From It?

The idea is that you purchase from a supplier that is specifically set up for dropshipping. These will be distributors who are not major brand wholesalers. Large brand wholesalers – such as Samsung or Apple, for example – will insist that merchants buy in bulk and have their own stock ready to send to customers. This gives the brand more control over their costs and revenue as well as working with certain channels that can best represent their brand. As a result, major brands will almost never work with dropshippers.

The suppliers that are set up for dropshipping tend to be distributors of smaller, lesser known brands. Although customers will probably not be familiar with the brand name, the advantage is that the products will be much cheaper as there is no huge label to boost the price. This means that the dropshipper can purchase the product at a low wholesale price, pay any shipping fees and add an additional margin of profit to the product and still provide an attractive price to the customer.

The amount of profit you make largely depends on what you sell. If you sell a highly popular product, there is a chance the market will be saturated and that the price competition will be hard to bet, especially for new entrants into the market that don't have a solid customer base already. Also, the cost of shipping fees means that profit margins, on the whole, remain quite thin. Selling to a niche segment of the market is the best bet as there is less competition and prices can afford to be a little higher, widening your profit margins.

The three main ways of increasing profits directly are:

> Increasing your prices. Check to see what your competition is charging and see how your prices compare. You can only increase profits as much as the market will tolerate.

> You can sell more volume. How you sell more will be largely influenced by your efforts of advertising and promotion, whether that's through a blog, social media, or any other way you can build up the exposure to the products you are selling.

> You can negotiate with your supplier to get a reduced handling fee. This will depend on the loyalty and relationship you and the supplier have. It will also depend on external costs such as the cost of shipping and the supplier's financial situation. There is no guarantee that they will lower their handling fee but it is something to consider after working with them for a while, especially if you can show you bring in plenty of orders.

The main advantage is that you will not be at much risk of losing much money as you aren't buying batches of stock that you may not sell. You can pay fees if you sell the product and then keep the profits to yourself.

An essential factor to consider with making profits with dropshipping is whether this process has a future or not. Research suggests it does and that dropshipping and e-commerce, in general, make up a continuously growing portion of all US retail sales. According to Forrester's Online Retail Forecast, online sales will account for 12.7% of all US retail sales by the end of 2017 and 17% by the end of 2022. At the end of the first quarter in 2017, e-commerce sales made up 8.5% of all retail sales; in other words, this is a total of $105.7 billion in sales. The market is huge.

The majority of dropshipping businesses are small ones, yet there are some that have grown to become highly successful such as Zappos and Wayfair. As mentioned before, price margins and volume of purchases are the most important when it comes to profits. Let's take a look at these two factors in more detail.

Merchants, or dropshippers, should aim for around 20% margins on their products with the minimum threshold at 15%. You can calculate your estimated profit by knowing your conversion rate. Your conversion rate is the number of visitors that go to your site (known as 'traffic') versus the number of those visitors that make a purchase. The average conversion rate for e-commerce businesses is 2.35% yet that can be lower or higher. Check your stats to get an accurate number, yet you can use this average to give you an idea of how much you will earn.

To check your site's profitability, use this equation:

(number of visitors to your site x 0.023) x (cost of average order x 0.20) = your estimated profit.

For example, if someone has an e-commerce store that sells fitness products. One of the core products is an exercise bike that is sold for $500. With a profit margin of 20%, the business owner would expect to make $100 on every sale. The site receives a total of 2,000 visitors per month so the conversion rate would assume that about 46 of those visitors will buy the exercise bike. If 46 people buy the exercise bike and the profit margin was $100 per purchase, the business owner makes a total of $4,600 profits.

Depending on what you sell, how much for, and what your profit margins are, you can make profits with dropshipping. The way you promote your product though is important and to get the conversion rates, you need to build a following. Two of the most common ways to do this is by blogging or creating a strong social media presence.

What Products Can You Sell With Dropshipping?

The variety of products is enormous, from clothes, electronics, and furniture to more niche products such as figure skating dresses and shower caps. While of course selling in a market that has a large audience, selling a product that can be found anywhere will reduce your chances of customers finding you amongst all the other competitors. Pick your niche product and do everything you can to meet that niche audience's needs to put you in a prime position. Although not necessary, a niche that you are genuinely interested in will help you too as you can impart your knowledge during the purchasing process – whether that's an informative caption to describe the product or blog posts leading to the product – creating the idea that you are a field expert. This will help your customers trust you and your product.

How can you find the best product for you to sell? First of all, thinking about your interests is a good start. If you're interested in something, no matter how unique, then there will be a group of others out there who are also interested in it. If it is a niche interest, such as fly fishing or cactus collecting, for example, consider what products you could see and how you can reach people who are in this market. If you love yoga, the market is already quite competitive, but you could find a niche even here with plus-sized yoga clothes or even yoga clothes for babies and children.

If all your interests are mainstream and you can't think of any niches that you could tap into, then check out large e-commerce stores such as eBay and Amazon. Spend some time searching through the hot trends on these platforms and make notes of their bestsellers. Try narrowing the bestselling items to a few niche areas – these could turn out to be great ideas for a dropshipping business. Check trends on Facebook, Instagram, and Twitter to see what people are talking about – perhaps a celebrity has started a new fashion trend of neon gym leggings or a diet that requires a specific, obscure kitchen utensil that is hard to find. It's moments like these that kind be temporarily quite profitable and ideal for the dropshipping as it doesn't require you to invest in a batch of products that may be hard to sell after the trend has faded.

Also, keep an eye on the calendar. The holiday season will bring plenty of opportunities to sell seasonal products – such as Halloween and Christmas – as well as sporting events and other moments of the year, like Valentine's Day, where niche and specific products become sought-after.

Is It Easy To Set Up A Dropshipping E-commerce Business?

For anyone that is at least a bit tech savvy, then it isn't too hard to get started. The main thing you need is to set up a website with a shopping cart. Alternatively, a virtual shop front on Amazon will work as well. If you already have a blog related to the product you will sell, that will help you a lot as you already should have an interested, engaged audience who could be interested in buying what you are selling. If you don't have a blog, it's a good idea to start one as this is where you can build up a community of trust and people that are within your target audience. Social media such as Facebook and Instagram play an important part in engaging with your potential customers and ultimately increasing conversion rates so make sure that you keep those accounts updated, stimulating, and active. If you don't have time to do it or are not sure how, either take a course about using social media for business or hire someone to do it. This will increase investment costs for you, but it can be worthwhile in the end when your conversion rate is up.

By using the dropshipping approach, you have more time to deal with your customers can lead them through the sale. Once they have made the purchase, you then put the responsibility into the hands of the supplier who sends the product to the customer. Some factors are worth noting about this though. First of all, as it is you that is the face of the business, if the customer is unsatisfied, you will have to deal with the refunds and return policy. It is in your long-term interests to have a fair refund policy in place and to stick to it to avoid negative feedback and unsatisfied customers that could spread bad reviews about your service. This is where it pays to know your supplier and what kind of products they are shipping as poor-quality products will reflect poorly on you.

Secondly, suppliers do charge a fee for this service as they want and need to make a profit too. This varies from supplier to supplier and depends on the product. On average, it's usually between $2 and $5. This is the handling fee which you will be charged, in addition to the wholesale cost of the item and then the overall cost of the shipping. These costs are essential to consider when working out your profit margins.

Will Customers Know That You Are A Dropshipping Business?

A good portion of e-commerce uses the dropshipping approach – it is estimated at between 20% and 30% - and most customers have no idea or even think about where the product is stocked. Those who work with online businesses may have more of an idea, yet dropshipping isn't considered a negative selling approach so even if a customer knew, they probably wouldn't be worried about it if the product meets their criteria and expectations and is sold at a price that suits their budget.

How To Pick A Supplier.

Picking a supplier with a good reputation is crucial, as the quality of their products and the speed of their delivery will ultimately reflect on you. Imagine you are a customer. You will want an easy to navigate website that provides you all the information that you need about the product you are thinking about purchasing. You want to be left with no doubts that this product will satisfy the very reason you want to buy it. Once you've made that purchase, you don't want to wait a long time to buy it and should you have any problems, you will want an easy to deal with customer service port of call.

Thinking like this will help you pick the best supplier. You need a supplier that will happily take back returns quickly and effectively as well as deals with refunds too. Excellent communication is key, as is excellent quality products. Testing the product is an effective way of knowing of its quality, and you can leave product reviews on your blog or site too to help customers in the purchase decision-making process. Do plenty of research, fact-check suppliers by reading reviews left by others on them, and ask people you know for an honest review of the product you want to sell. If others like it, you will probably do well selling it.

Some of the most popular and largest suppliers for dropshipping business are Oberlo and Shopify. These are both trusted and reputable sites.

However, it still pays to ask questions about your supplier, whoever it is. A lousy supplier can destroy your business, so make an effort from the beginning to know who your supplier is and how they can add value to your company.

Here are some points to consider before partnering with a potential supplier:

➢ Check delivery times. This includes how long it takes to process the order and how long it will take to arrive at the customer's house or address once it has been shipped.

➢ Check if the supplier has a tracking system. Some customers like to see the status of the order, and this can be a unique selling point for you. It will also help in the event of any lost orders.

➢ The shipping methods are critical, especially if some of your customers or even the supplier itself are based overseas. Things such as using UPS and FedEx are essential, as is the possibility of overnight delivery.

➢ Check to see if the supplier's products come with warranties and guarantees, something especially important if you are selling electronics. Finding out what the supplier will do if the product fails is critical as whatever happens, the customer will be ready to blame you, and not the supplier, if something goes wrong.

➢ Ask the supplier about their policy in the case of lost shipments.

What are the advantages of dropshipping?

➢ The financial risk is far smaller than setting up a traditional retail business where you would need to invest in a considerable sum of money in a stock that has no guarantee of being sold. With dropshipping, you don't need to purchase any products until a purchase has is made. This means setting up a dropshipping business is quite easy and not that risky.

➢ Not having to deal with any actual physical products is a significant advantage. You don't need to store anything in a warehouse and avoid the costs and risks of doing so. You also don't need to pack and send your orders, record inventory levels, handle returns (only your customer's complaint!), reorder products, and finally, you don't have to do any stock management.

> You can run a dropshipping business from anywhere. Your only requirements are a strong internet connection and a means of communication with your customers. The location issues associated with a bricks and mortar store are completely removed.

> You can stock several items on your site at no additional cost. Your only concern is if your supplier sells a particular product. If they do, then you can too.

> Dropshipping has a low overhead as you don't have the cost of stock or managing a physical store and warehouse.

> The fact that the supplier takes care of processing and shipping the purchase makes it far easier to scale a dropshipping business as the workload will not be as much, even if the number of sales increases dramatically.

What are the drawbacks?

> Competitive areas make gaining profits hard, and low margins of profit are a common characteristic among highly sought-after products. Therefore working from a niche segment is vital.

> The inventory levels at your supplier's end may not be updated with the information you have. This can lead you to sell a product that is not actually available.

Finding technology to sync the supplier with your site is essential.

➤ Using multiple suppliers can lead to differences in shipping costs which can leave a bad impression on the customer if they are being charged different prices for the same shipping. After all, they don't necessarily know that the product is coming from various suppliers. Even if they did, they would still expect the same shipping costs. It also gets confusing trying to calculate these differences on your site.

➤ If a supplier makes a mistake and the customer is angry, you have to take the blame.

Is It Worth It?

Dropshipping isn't perfect, but if planned carefully, it can make a highly profitable business, especially when added to an already successful blog that is generating plenty of traffic. However, even without a blog or an online presence, it is entirely possible to build a dropshipping business with some time and effort.

Chapter Summary

In this chapter, we looked at dropshipping and what it is.

- Dropshipping is a type of supply chain process where the merchant buys the stock from the supplier only after a customer has made a purchase. This means that the store never has inventory in stock and it only buys it as and when is needed.

- It is a less capital-heavy type of store and has far less risk than the traditional model of buying in bulk and trying to sell it.
- The lower risk and small capital investment are two huge advantages. The disadvantages are mainly related to narrow margins if competing in a competitive market.
- If done correctly and carefully, it can be a highly profitable way of making money.

In the next chapter we will look in more detail at Shopify, a form of dropshipping.

Chapter Two: How To Use Shopify For Dropshipping

In this chapter, we will look at how you can use Shopify for dropshipping.

What is Shopify?

Shopify is an excellent platform for those looking to set up an online store to sell their own products or to start a dropshipping store. This e-commerce platform offers straightforward ways to organize your products, customise the face of your store, accept and process payments, track orders, and communicate with your customers. It provides solutions for anyone selling anything, anywhere, such as social media, on a blog, in a physical store, or even from a stand in your garden.

Its versatility is its strongest selling point as it is suitable for small business as well as large ones and offers a solid platform for a broad range of industries. If you are setting up your first online e-commerce, then Shopify is a safe bet as its straightforward procedures, and easy navigation will make it a straightforward process.

What can you sell on Shopify?

You can sell anything on Shopify, as long as it's not illegal. There is a section on their site labeled 'E-commerce by Industry' that lists their most popular categories. These include food products, e-books, art, fashion items, furniture, and a whole list of other items.

How To Set Up A Dropshipping Store On Shopify.

Before you set up a store, it's good to create a logo that represents your brand. This will be the first thing customers notice and will give your business a professional look. You can make a professional-looking logo using a freelancer on Fiverr for around $20 (although it can be much less or much more).

The great thing about Shopify is that you can build a dropshipping site on its platform for little initial investment and in less than a day. It means you can quickly start selling your products, even if you have no prior experience of building websites. The site is clean and easy to use. Here's how you can set up your online store with Shopify.

➢ You can start on Shopify with a 14-day free trial. You need to fill out your details on the Shopify site and add your store name. If your store name is already in use by someone else, then you can't move forward, and you will have to think of another name. After, you will be required to provide information about your business such as its size, what stage it's at, and what you will be selling. Then you can click on 'Add Online Store'. This will take you back to the homepage, but you will see on the left side of the screen that there is a tab with 'Online Store'. This is your new e-commerce store.

> Buying a web domain sooner rather than later is vital as your store will instantly look legitimate and professional. If you don't buy a domain, then you face the risk of someone else buying it before you. Also, you Shopify URL will look this: yourstorename.myshopify.com. Having your own domain will get rid of the 'myshopify' part. This is not only important to give a good impression to your customers, but to your suppliers as well. To buy a new domain, simply click on the 'Online Store' then 'Domains' and finally, 'Buy new domain'. You can check availability and then purchase it. It costs $13 for one year.

> Next, it is a good idea to set up email forwarding. This means that when a customer emails you at the Shopify email address (info@yourbusinessname), it will automatically go to an email address of your choice. This is important as Shopify isn't hosting your emails. When you reply to a forwarded email, it will come from the account the email was delivered to. Shopify will set up two accounts for you – info@yourbusinessname and sales@yourbusinessname. It's a great idea to set up one for customerservice@yourbusinessname or

help@yourbusinessname, so customers feel their inquiry is going to the right place.

➢ Building your dropshipping store on Shopify's platform is easy. One great advantage as well is that the platform is both desktop and mobile friendly. To create your shopfront, you need to choose a theme from Shopify's collection. There are both free and premium themes, with the latter priced at around $150 or more. Once you have installed your theme, you can customise it.

➢ Next, you need to add a few pages to your store. These will include a homepage, an 'about us' section (this is important to allow the customer to get a feel for who you are), a 'product page', a 'returns' page, a 'shipping' page, and finally, a 'contact us' page.

➢ Now you have your store. Next, you want to start adding your products. You can use the information and images from your supplier's site. You can add in tags for each product to help make it easier for customers to find. When adding related products, you can duplicate the page and edit specific bits of information, making it much easier to upload new product descriptions.

➢ Once you have your products on the site, the layout of the pages becomes much clearer. Now is a good time to fine-tune your store by tweaking its appearance and adding your social media pages.

➢ Shopify has plenty of additional apps and plug-ins that you can add to your store. Some of free, some are priced. The first one you should add is a customer review app as this lets customers leave feedback about your products. This is vital for new customers who often rely on what others say to make the final step in the purchase decision-making process.

➢ After your 14-day trial period, you will need to start paying for Shopify. The plans are monthly although there are annual and biennial as well which give discounts on price (10% and 20% respectively). You can upgrade or downgrade whenever you want, and you can cancel whenever you want too. Four plans range from $14 to $179 per month. The basic plan – at $29 – is fine for a new dropshipping business.

➢ The last thing to do is to add your payment details so you can get paid and fill in the meta description, so your store appears in search results.

Chapter Summary

In this chapter, we looked at how you can use Shopify to set up your own dropshipping business.

- Shopify is a site that provides a complete platform for your online store, including payment processing and storefront designs.

- It's easy to set up, and you can have your store completed in less than a day for less than $50 (a little more if you create a logo too).

In the next chapter, we will look at how you can make money on Kindle publishing.

Chapter Three: How To Make A Business With Kindle Publishing

In this chapter, we will look at how you can do an online business with Amazon Kindle Publishing.

What is Amazon Kindle Publishing?

The publishing platform provides a straightforward way for practically anyone to publish their own e-books online and have autonomy over the way in which they are sold. Effectively, it allows anyone to be both an author and a publisher. Gone were the days of months of writing a book and pitching it to editors. Now, books can be uploaded on the platform for immediate sale to a global audience, creating a lucrative means of passive income.

Thousands of people are using Kindle to make money yet there is still a large audience waiting to be catered for, bringing plenty of opportunities to fill niches. The difference between making a few dollars per month to thousands of dollars depends on what topics you write about, how you are perceived as an author, and finally, how you promote your work.

Selling in an already saturated market – areas such as dieting and travel – will be far harder to generate high income than publishing for a niche audience. Selecting a niche is the best way of making money. There are fewer competitors, and you have a better chance of building a following and establishing yourself as the best author and leader in that field. The lack of resources in particular niches means availability and choices are slim, giving a much higher chance that your book will be chosen over others.

If you want to publish in a heavily competed market, then you need a clear and robust strategy. The most important thing is to establish yourself as an expert or authority in this field. You can do this by building a community following through answering questions on Quora or writing regular, expert articles in a blog. People will recognize your name and want to learn more from your books. If you have no background in a field and people can't find you online, your book is likely to become swallowed up by more competitive players in such a fierce market.

How to make money on the Kindle Publishing platform

To sell a book, you need a book to sell. Don't worry if writing is not your strong point. A secret of the e-book industry is that the author does not actually write the many of the books sold online. Instead, they are written by ghostwriters who write about the topic based on a client brief and then sell the book along with all copyrights to the publisher. This means that the publisher can put their own name on the cover and say they are the author. For a relatively small fee (this largely depends on which company you use), you can get a professionally edited book, fully formatted, and with a Kindle book cover in a couple of weeks. It will then be ready to publish and sell.

The key to ghostwriting is choosing the right company. This is vital as this book will have your name on it, and if customers complain about the writing, it is you they will blame. Hot Ghost Writers, for example, is a reputable company that provides a range of services from fully formatted e-books to physical books.

The title is something you should carefully consider. Search for the main SEO words (Search Engine Optimisation) relating to your topic and include them in the title. This will make your book more search engine-friendly and make a dramatic difference to whether potential customers can find your book or not.

Now that you have your book ready, it's prepared for the next stage which is uploading it onto the Kindle platform and getting it published for your audience to buy.

Here are all the steps you need to set up the Kindle publishing platform:

> ➤ Head to the KDP (Kindle Direct Publishing) website. Even if you already have an Amazon account, you will need to create a new username and password on KDP. The two sites and account are kept separate.

> ➤ Next fill out all your details, including your bank account so you can receive money and put in your tax information. The tax section is more difficult to set up so we'll look at this step by step.

Amazon will send you a report on all the income you earned on their platform and any tax withheld. They send this at the end of the fiscal year, and it's known as the W-2 form. This will help you with your tax returns, as all sales and royalties made on Amazon must be reported.

The tricky part is the withholding fee. If you are a US citizen or have a US tax number, simply put in your tax details and KDP will verify them. If you have a tax number from a different country, Amazon may hold onto up to 30% of all your earnings for tax purposes. To prevent this, send Amazon an ID number that proves you don't live in the US and then the withholding rate will be reduced.

The amount withheld will depend on the country. The UK, for example, has a 0% withholding rate as the UK and the US have a tax treaty. This means Amazon won't hold onto any of your income. Some countries have more complicated treaties so even if you provide ID, Amazon may still hold onto some of your income. It's best to check this on the platform so you know what to expect regarding how much you will earn and how much will be deducted.

> Once your personal details and tax information are in the system, you are ready to publish your book. In the main section of the platform that you will use is 'bookshelf' where all your books are stored and where you add new titles.

> From the 'bookshelf', you can upload your new book. Make sure you select 'worldwide rights'. This will make sure that your book is protected in all the countries

where the Kindle e-books are sold. In other words, it ensures that no-one can copy your work.

➢ Now, you can choose your royalties. Your options are either 35% royalties or 70% royalties. Selecting 70% royalties may seem like the most obvious option, but there are some reasons why 35% is necessary.

First, if your book is priced outside the range of $2.99 to $9.99, you cannot earn 70% royalties. For example, if you want to sell your book for $2, you can only get 35% royalties as the 70% won't be available for you.

Opting for 35% royalties is better if your book file size is large. This is because when your book is selected for 70% royalties, you will be required to pay for download fees. This costs around $0.15 per MB of the file so it can be expensive if your book is big. If you opt for 35% royalties, however, you don't need to pay for download fees. Check the file size of your book before you choose which royalties to have to make sure you are getting the best deal.

There are a couple of other things to be aware of when you opt for 70% royalties. Your book can't be available in public domain. Also, when you select 70% royalties, you agree that a buyer can lend copies of their purchased copy to anyone they want. Naturally you will think that this means a loss of sales, but, allowing buyers to lend your book to others can be a positive thing. Not only does it give your book free exposure, but it also helps encourage more book reviews (which means you will rank higher on Amazon) and build long-term relations with potential future buyers.

➢ After selecting the royalties, you need to choose the price you want to sell it for. Most authors choose between $2.99 and $9.99. If you are a new publisher, giving away the first book for a limited time for free is a good strategy to build up an audience and develop your reputation. If you are already established online with a strong community following you, you can get away with charging immediately and setting a price that matches your audience's expectations.

➢ Now your book is priced and set to go. Click save and then publish. Your book is now on the global e-book market waiting to be bought. You are now both an author and a publisher.

However, the book won't sell itself. Now the book is online, your job as a marketer begins. You have to promote your book and give a reason for people to buy it. The easiest step is to ask friends and family to read it. Ask them to leave reviews. As we looked at before, the more positive reviews you have, the higher you will rank on Amazon. Use your blog – if you have one – to promote it. Now is the time to get social media-savvy and use it as much as possible to get your book out there. Try making a creative campaign to get people sharing your promotion. It doesn't have to be anything fancy, just something that will appeal to your audience and make them want to buy it and share it.

Your first book is the first step to building a successful online business. Aim to become a reputable author and an important source of information in your chosen area to make sure you bring value to your market and get your audience to trust you. Once your first book is online, the rest will follow like a snowball;

building up a bigger e-book platform and creating a larger and continuous stream of passive income.

Chapter Summary

In this chapter, we looked at how to build an online business with Kindle Publishing and make profits from this potentially lucrative platform.

- Amazon Kindle Publishing is an online platform known as KDP (Kindle Direct Publishing) where anyone can publish a book online. It has become a trendy way of creating an online business and can create a steady passive income stream.

- It's important to choose the right niche to sell in, and this niche may not always be the area that you are passionate about. Ideally, it would be, but it's not a problem if not. Areas such as dieting and travel are heavily saturated and become much harder to sell. However, find a niche – such as traveling with disabilities or yoga for children – and you have far less competition and more chance of selling your books.

- If you're not a budding writer or simply don't have time to do it yourself, use a ghostwriter to write your books. Make sure you upload your book later on the publishing platform with the correct tax information, the right royalties, and your desired selling price.

- Your book won't sell itself and promotion is a key factor in getting it exposure and letting your target audience know that there is a book that will meet their needs.

In the next chapter, we will look at how to make money freelancing. A lot of freelancing work is done online and offers a great way to make money on a flexible schedule. We will also look at some of the best and most profitable freelancing jobs on the current market.

Chapter Four: Finding Freelance Work

In this chapter, we will look at the world of freelancing.

Freelancing is slightly different to being self-employed, yet the two terms overlap and being self-employed is technically a freelancer too. When you're self-employed, you have your own company and perhaps some employees who you delegate tasks to. On the other hand, a freelancer is someone who works for themselves and has no employees; rather, they are their own unique entity. Freelancers sell their unique skills as a service, such as writing, design, or web development, among many other categories. Freelancers tend to build up a network of loyal clients that they work with to generate a steady, consistent income and do the odd job here and there with one-time clients.

Like with anything, freelancing has its perks and downsides. Some of the advantages include:

➤ You can say when enough is enough. As a freelancer, you can control your own workload, and if you feel you have taken on too much, you can drop a project or refuse to accept any more. Surprisingly, this can take discipline as it is not always so easy to know when to stop, but at least as your own boss, you can decide when you are feeling the strain and need to cut back.

➤ Freelancing is demanding work at times, yet you can decide when you take a break and enjoy the privilege of an afternoon nap. This can help with productivity as you allow your brain to recharge regularly which allows you to think more clearly.

➤ You are location-independent. If you want to work at home, you can. If that new coffee shop down the road has caught your eye, you can work there as long as it has wi-fi. If you want to spend a few months abroad and travel spontaneously, you can. Being freelance gives you the flexibility to work wherever you want, as long as you have wi-fi.

➤ You have a flexible schedule. As long as you meet your deadlines, you can work whenever you want. Whether you are more productive first thing in the morning or late at night, you can carve out your schedule to suit your needs.

➤ You can dedicate your working life to building a skill that you really enjoy. For example, if you want to be a writer, you can focus on being your own success in that area and build some excellent clients that will want you to write for them. You can end up working in a job that you really love and so that oft-heard phrase of 'work with your passion and you will never work again' really becomes true.

There are some downsides though:

- If you are someone that has to work with other people, you may find freelancing lonely. Most freelancers work alone, yet some try to work in co-working spaces to at least be surrounded by other people. This can be a fantastic way to meet fellow freelancers and be with like-minded people.

- You need to have self-motivation and time management skills of iron. It's all too easy to slip into a relaxed mood when you work as a freelancer and lull yourself into a false sense of security that you have all the time in the world to meet a deadline. However, that deadline comes quicker than you can imagine and you need to learn how to prepare for that. As a freelancer, you depend on your clients for your income, and if you can't meet their expectations and start losing customers, it becomes tricky to rebuild your reputation and find new ones. Organising your schedule is essential and a task that should never be overlooked.

- If you travel, you won't have holiday pay. Also, if you're sick, you won't get sick pay. You need to save up for this moments. Finally, having a pension is becoming less and less likely in the younger generation – such as generation Y and younger - who are more likely to be freelancers than older segments of the population. You may need to prepare yourself to be working much longer than what is the norm nowadays.

➤ Unless you can secure contracts with clients, you may find yourself relying on an unpredictable monthly income where the amount fluctuates dramatically month by month.

Despite the drawbacks, the freelance lifestyle is an attractive one and continues to entice people to it in growing numbers. Freelance can be highly profitable too depending on the area you work in and your reputation in the area you are offering skills in. Here are the ten top-paying freelance jobs. The rates vary depending on company and location, so the list is in no order.

➤ Translator. Translators can earn a very high income, depending on level. Sworn translators, who must undergo vigorous testing and studies, translate official documents and can earn a comfortable income. Pairs such as English-Spanish and English-French are extremely competitive and are best accompanied with formal university education. Less common pairs with languages considered important for business or trade are the most sought-after such as native English with Arabic, Mandarin, or Russian.

➤ Financial writer. Given the technical nature of finance, someone that can both understand financial talk and write succinctly is an asset. Many financial writers put together financial analysis or market commentaries. They may also write annual reports, newsletters, and compile books.

➢ Infographic designer. As the world is becoming more complex and in need of information fast, infographics are becoming a popular way of showcasing and presenting important data. Companies need people who have a creative flair coupled with technical skills and will pay good money for someone to capture complex information and lay it out in a simple yet impacting infographic.

➢ Web designer and developer. More and more people are looking to make money through blogging (we'll come to that in a bit) which requires more than free theme on WordPress. Many bloggers want a user-friendly site that captures their brand and looks incredible. Web designers who can present a portfolio that shows not only their technical skill of making a site but can also showcase how well they understand visuals and brands, will find themselves in great demand for website building.

➢ Blogging. Making money on a blog is not an overnight thing and takes time before you can run it full time. However, it can be done if you are blogging about something that appeals to carefully designed niche and results in a high volume of traffic. Bloggers make money through sponsored posts, affiliate marketing, selling e-books, and advertising, among other income streams. The monthly income varies enormously from a few dollars to thousands of dollars per month. This is largely dependent on what you are blogging about and how much effort and energy you pour into it.

➢ Social media manager. There is a growing wave of companies outsourcing social media tasks to freelancers, and consequently, the amount of freelance social media managers has grown. Social media managers take care of a company's social network such as Instagram, Facebook, Pinterest, and Twitter. They keep the accounts active, they post regularly, they create campaigns, they respond to customers, they interact with their feed, and they constantly build, represent, and boost the brand. A good social media manager needs experience and the ability to show they understand the brand's voice and, most importantly, translate that onto several social media platforms in a consistent style.

➢ Programmer. The most sought-after programmers are software and mobile app development. To get a foothold in this competitive yet highly lucrative market, you need to show you have master-like skills in coding. This will be beyond doing a couple of free online courses and will require evidence of formal training and experience. Some freelancers earn hundreds of dollars an hour as programmers while others can reach beyond one thousand dollars an hour. Having a solid skill set in a programming language such as iOS and WebGL will give you a competitive edge.

➢ Content writing. The importance of online marketing trends is most visible in the growth of content writers who do blogging work for businesses and develop catchy, engaging content that companies can use on their site to help entice customers. Content writing is more than just writing a few articles. It has to capture the style of the company and reflect the brand as well as provide immense value for the customer that reads it.

➢ Graphic design. Graphic designers are in high demand as more people want specialized, customised, and standout logos for their brands, blogs, and sites. The graphic design market is quite competitive with many designers entering the market with little experience yet offering attractive low prices. To get into the high brackets, you need a cracking portfolio that shows your creative skills, your eye for details, and your ability to capture the essence of a brand. If you have this, there will be people who are more than willing to pay handsomely for your services.

➢ Video editor. The way people consume information is slowly changing from written content to videos. Although written articles are still by far the most popular, the number of videos being watched cannot be ignored and provides another channel for companies to reach their audience. People who have the technical skills of creating great videos and an eye for knowing what people want can earn a steady and comfortable income as a video editor.

These are some of the most popular and profitable freelance jobs. However, you can turn almost any skill into a freelance position with some careful planning and promoting. For example, if you are a secretary or a personal assistant, you can repurpose these skills to become a freelance and online virtual assistant where you take care of businesses day-to-day online. You would need to set up a website that promotes your services and build up clients from there. Or, if you are an accountant, you can offer your skills online by managing the accounts of other online businesses. The scope of online work is huge, and it's possible to find ways to turn a nine-to-five job into a more flexible position.

So, you have an excellent idea for a job that you can turn freelance. How do you go about getting clients? Your own blog is a good start as people will want to see your work and learn more about you. Update a blog regularly with fascinating content and informative articles, and people will be more likely to return to your site and consider you in the future should they need your services. It also acts as a portfolio for your work, so you have something to showcase to prospective clients. Make your blog or site as clean and user-friendly as possible to create a good user experience for visitors.

There are also platforms where you can advertise your skills and services to the market. With these platforms, you can apply for jobs directly and open your profile so others can contact you for your services. Here are some of the best and most popular platforms.

> **Upwork.** One of the biggest platforms right now for freelance work, Upwork has around 12 million freelancers and 5 million clients registered on its site. It is estimated that approximately three million jobs are posted there each year so the potential of finding work there is huge. There are all sorts of work on there such as technical writing, translation, and web development. Once you have a loyal client base, finding new work becomes easier, and potential clients can see how you rate based on

past feedback from other customers. You can also take tests on the platform to showcase your skill set and give yourself a competitive edge over the others. Once you have a firm foothold on the platform, you can make significant money. The problem is getting started. You need to prove your credentials to clients as competition is fierce. Because of high competition, the clients' budget tends to be low as they can find reasonable work for a low cost. However, some clients are willing to pay more for quality work, and it's your job to show them that you can do this.

➢ **Fiverr.** This platform is a global marketplace with a vast range of services on offer, starting from $5 upwards, which is where the company got its name from. There are more than three million services on its site that range between $5 and $500, so profits are there for the experienced freelancer. Like Upwork, competition is fierce, especially in areas such as graphic design where dozens of designers charge just $5 for a logo, making it hard to get work if you charge more. Consider finding a niche to make yourself stand out and accumulate a strong portfolio to give yourself an edge. The work may start off slowly until you build a large client base, but once you get there, you should be able to generate a good income stream and have a painless way to find new clients.

➢ **Toptal.** Whereas anyone who wants to be a freelancer can apply to work on Upwork and Fiverr, Toptal is far more selective. A vigorous screening process means that only the best freelancers are chosen to work on the platform, and with clients such as JP Morgan and Airbnb, the potential earnings are appealing. There is also the chance for freelancers to join the Toptal community which has regular meetups and technology events that you can attend and network. The primary areas they look for freelancers is developers, designers, and financial experts.

➢ **99designs.** 99designs is specifically for freelance designers and is especially suited for more experienced and highly talented designers. The platform allows designers to compete in design contests where clients give feedback and select the best ones. If you are talented, it's a fantastic way to showcase your skills and get picked on talent rather than just the lowest bid.

➢ **Freelance Writing Gigs**. Finding freelance writing work can be challenging as competition is fierce, and publications or businesses tend to want someone with a proven track record. Freelance Writing Gigs has plenty of opportunities for writers, blogs, editors, and publishers and have both entry-level and more experienced work available. It's an excellent way to get an extra income through writing for more seasoned writers and for new writers to find a gig that will get their first published piece.

➢ **Facebook groups.** Search for groups on Facebook using keywords such as 'remote jobs', 'travel jobs', and 'freelance jobs'. Not only will you get to meet like-minded people, companies, and other members regularly post opportunities on there for both long-term work and one-off projects.

Here are some tips for making money as a freelancer and turning this into your unique stream of income.

- Choose your niche. If you want to be a writer, what kind of writer. If you're going to be a programmer, specify your skills. This is important as clients like to work with someone that they feel is an expert, rather than someone who is good at a little bit of everything.

- Define who your client is and what solution they are looking for. This will help you tailor your services to meet your ideal audience and provide value to customers.

- Having a high quality, clean website is vital to showcase your services and provide a list of client testimonials. By having a professional looking site, it reflects better on you and what you are offering.

- Before diving straight into the world of freelancing, it is good to stick to your full-time job and start building your freelance portfolio. This will include developing the site, your social media pages, and creating a high-quality portfolio. By keeping your full-time job and developing the freelance work on the side, you still have a steady stream of income while building your own client base of profitable, loyal customers. It means you can be more selective about who you work with as you are not in desperate need of money. A good moment to leave your full-time job is when your freelance work is bringing in enough money to support your lifestyle. It will be a lot of challenging work juggling two jobs in the beginning, but it will pay off in the end.

➤ To get yourself out there and expose your work, you need to build a good reputation and credibility in your area. Write an e-book, give a speech at public events, or develop an excellent source of information about your area in a blog. The key is to show people that you know what you are talking about and to distinguish yourself as someone worth working with.

➤ Set your prices to match the value you offer. Don't be shy about charging higher rates. Customers are happy to pay more for what they think is a high-quality service, so make a pristine first impression and make sure that you deliver what you promise. If you do this, then you can maintain higher prices.

➤ In addition to writing regularly on your own blog, do guest posts in your area for other websites. This helps increase your exposure and get your name out there. You can link your guest posts back to your website so people can easily find you and discover more about your services.

Chapter Summary

In this chapter, we looked at the world of freelancing and how you can become a freelancer.

- Freelancing comes with several significant advantages such as being location-independent and the flexibility to work on your own schedule. You can also work in an area that you feel genuinely passionate about and can focus on making yourself an expert in that area. The downsides include no holiday pay, sickness pay, or pension, and you have to be extremely disciplined, self-motivated, and pro-active to stick to your goals and build your client base.

- You can be a freelancer in almost any area. Some of the most common include content writers, social media managers, web developer, and designer.

- You can find work on online platforms. Sites such as Upwork and Fiverr post millions of jobs and can be an excellent option to start building your experience and portfolio.

In the next chapter, we will look at how you can build and create online courses to earn a good passive income.

Chapter Five: Making Online Courses

In this chapter, we will look at how you can build a passive income by making and selling online courses.

Among the many ways of making money online, an online course can be one of the most profitable. Global Industry Analysts, Inc predict that online learning will reach a market value of more than $240 billion by 2021. The scope and potential are enormous.

The wonderful thing about creating your own online course is that you don't necessarily need to be an expert in a subject. You just need to have a solid foundation of knowledge about the area. There are courses available online for practically all topics nowadays, such as web development, languages, personal development, cooking, photography, and childcare. Although there are thousands of courses being sold online, the market is not saturated, and some people have managed to make thousands of dollars per month from selling courses.

Feeling inspired? Here's how to make your own online course.

➢ Choose a topic. You should choose a topic that relates to something you are good at as it's easier to draw from your experience and knowledge than to research a topic entirely from scratch. Think about a hobby or a skill you are good at. If you write articles, a course about how to structure an article, how to interview subjects, or how to pitch to editors are some ideas. If you love playing snooker, you could have a course on snooker for beginnings, for example. The scope is wide, and you have plenty of room to find a topic. The more niche your course is though, the better.

➢ Once you've decided a topic for your course, make sure you research the market to see if people would buy it. You may think it is a great idea but perhaps your audience wouldn't pay money to learn about it. Ask friends, family, and post in forums to gauge an idea of how popular your course could be.

➢ You need to outline the bare bones of the course so you can see the content you need to provide and the information you need to put in. The course must be in-depth and offer real value for your customers by giving them the information they couldn't find anywhere else. Divide your course into lessons and modules so the module would be the broad subject and the lesson would go into more details.

➢ You should consider how you will teach your lessons. Will it be articles, videos, audios, or worksheets? Will you do step by step instructions or a series of explanatory videos? Consider the best way to deliver the information that you're providing and try to think what would be best for the customer. You want to create something that is user-friendly, informative, and digestible.

➢ Now is the fun part; creating the lessons. It's also the most time-consuming. Not only should you think about how the lessons are presented, but you should consider things such as having a logo and having a consistent color theme. Make sure you proof-read it and that the videos have no glitches. Consider paying for a proof-reader or ask a friend or family member to look it over for you.

➢ Once your course has been made and thoroughly checked over for any slips or mistakes, then it's time to sell it. Now is the moment that you have to decide where to sell your course. One way is to sell it on your own site, especially one that gets a lot of traffic. There are plugins you can add to your site to allow it to support a course and payment. If you prefer a ready-made platform, then use a site such as Udemy or SkillShare. Both these sites allow people to upload their course and sell it on their platform. Just be aware that they will take a fee of each sale that you make. Other popular platforms include Teachable and Ruzuku. Check the conditions of each site, but most don't retain exclusive rights so you can sell the course on multiple platforms.

➢ Now your course is online and ready for the world to buy it, you have to start marketing it. You could have the best course in the world, but if people don't know about it, you will never sell it in the numbers that you want. The easiest way to start is to tell all your friends and family about it. Use your social media pages to share the course link and ask people you know to share it too. If you have a website, advertise your course there and use all your business social media pages also. It's worth paying for Facebook ads and offering an initial discounted price to sell it at to entice more people to buy it. This will help you build up reviews and feedback, which is essential to make other people want to buy the course.

➢ Make sure you update your course from time to time to make sure that the information remains current and timely. This is an excellent strategy to resell it as well by advertising the newly updated course.

You don't need to sell only one course in one area. You can develop multiple courses in different areas. If you are selling a great course, you can build up a comfortable income stream. The initial effort of making the course will reward you by bringing in a continuous passive income.

Let's look at some of the platforms available to sell your courses on and what makes them special. These are some of the most popular and well-known.

➢ **Udemy.** This online platform has thousands of courses offering both teaching and learning opportunities. There is an extraordinary range of topics from managing social media to learning a new language. There are about 16 million students across the world using Udemy, so there is a tremendous potential to sell courses. The platform is free to use although Udemy takes a cut of the total sales you make. This ranges from 3% to 75%, depending on the way in which the course was sold. For example, if the sale came through Udemy's own marketing, they will take 50% of the sales. The best kind of course for Udemy is one that is a minimum of 30 minutes, although many are several hours long. Prices for courses range from $20 to $200.

➢ **Skillshare.** Like Udemy, SkillShare has thousands of courses with hundreds of different topics such as business, personal development, art, and photography. To upload a course, you need to make the classes at how and then upload it using SkillShare's class creation tool. You earn money from the number of minutes a student watches your class per month. There is also a referral programme where you earn an additional $10 for every student you bring to the site that signs up for the premium account. You level of income can vary. SkillShare says that on average, the teachers make $3,000 per year, yet some are making around $40,000 per year. Not bad for a passive income stream.

➢ **Thinkific.** This platform allows you to create your own course on your site. So rather than your course being on a separate host, you get to have the course advertised on your site. This is far easier for your visitors to see your course. You have more flexibility on how you make your course and what price you charge. You also get to keep 100% of the sale. You must pay a fee though to sign up for Thinkific, although the starter plan is for free and had basic features. If you want more advanced tools, you will need to pay. The most expensive program is $279 per month, yet this is best for large companies that have courses for groups or cross-functional teams.

Here are some of the advantages of making an online course to create a stream of income.

> ➢ It's straightforward to make your own online course nowadays with some many available platforms to upload it and sell it. It is also easy to market your course thanks to social media and increased platforms of advertising.
> ➢ You can make a course to pad out your income. It can also be used as another service that you offer your clients on top of what your current business does. For example, if you have a lifestyle blog, you could create a makeup tutorial course that expands on article posts you already have and goes into more detail.
>
> ➢ It is a potentially highly profitable passive income stream that means you will earn money with little maintenance once it is online.
>
> ➢ Your course will be available to a global audience as it is online.

As with almost everything, there are some drawbacks to making an online course.

➢ Creating it, especially if you use videos which require editing, can be time-consuming.

➢ Using a host server such as SkillShare or Udemy means that you must pay a fee to the platform for every sale you make.

➢ Having an online course is not a guarantee that you will make money. It mostly depends on how well you advertise it, the quality of your course, the needs of the market, and how well you can reach your target audience.

Chapter Summary

In this chapter, we looked at how you can make money from selling online courses.

➢ Making an online course is easier than ever, especially as there are platforms online where you can upload and sell your classes, complete with a payment solution.

➢ You don't necessarily need to be an expert in a subject to sell a course. You just need to be knowledgeable about the topic and be able to provide value to your customers.

➢ Done correctly and selling online courses can be a great way of making a passive income.

In the next chapter, we will look at how to make money using cryptocurrency trading and investing.

Chapter Six: Making Money With Cryptocurrency Trading And Investing

In this chapter, we will look at how you can make money trading and investing in cryptocurrency.

In contrast to fiat money, which is your regular money such as dollars and pounds, cryptocurrency is a global form of digital money. It exists virtually and is embedded in cryptography technology which a process of transforming standard information into a complex code that is practically impossible to decipher. This code is used to make transfers and track the movement of cryptocurrency, making it highly secure and difficult to hack.

One of the most well-known cryptocurrencies is Bitcoin that was the first cryptocurrency to be created. Launched in 2009, Bitcoin remains the best known and most popular one on the market, despite sharing an arena with more than 900 other types of cryptocurrencies. Some of the other popular cryptocurrencies include Ethereum, Monero, Litecoin, and Ripple.

So, how does cryptocurrency work?

Cryptocurrencies operate on a decentralized technological platform called the blockchain. This means users can store their cryptocurrencies and make payments online without the need for an intermediary, such as a bank or financial institution. Each transaction is validated by miners, people who operate computers to process blocks of transactions using highly complex mathematical problems. All transactions are registered on the public ledger or the blockchain. This means all users can see every single transaction ever performed.

Cryptocurrency has some key characteristics.

> All transactions are irreversible. This means that once you send a payment, there is no way to reverse it. This also means that it is vital that you triple check who you are sending your money to as if you send it to the wrong account, there is no way to get it back.

> The cryptocurrency accounts are anonymous, and the users' identities are kept a secret. Hence why, if you accidentally send your funds to the wrong account, you can't get it back as you won't know who to speak with. Every account and transaction is recorded and registered to a random combination of characters known as addresses.

> Cryptocurrency transactions operate on a global scale and connect all corners of the world. There are no issues with exchange rates, and transactions can happen

almost instantly, although this depends on the currency. Bitcoin can still take up to 20 minutes for a transaction to be confirmed.

➢ The world of cryptocurrency is extremely secure as the technology it is built on is practically impossible to decipher. Owners have private keys like PIN numbers, and they need these to confirm and make transactions.

➢ Anyone can use cryptocurrency, and it doesn't discriminate on the financial background. Once you have bought some cryptocurrency coins, you can start trading them.

So, how can you make money on trading and investing in cryptocurrency?

Like regular fiat money, cryptocurrency value rises and drops depending on market conditions. For those who invested in Bitcoin in 2010 would have made a significant profit on the currency if you compare the value to what it is now. In 2010, one Bitcoin was worth around $0.08. Nowadays, in 2017 it is worth over $4,500 per Bitcoin. For those who took the initiative and sought first-mover advantages, certainly made the right move when buying Bitcoin in its early stages.

The key to making money on cryptocurrency is to invest in a coin whose value will continue to rise. When it reaches the desired value that you have in mind, then is the best time to sell it or trade it for another currency. Although Bitcoin is older now, it still has enormous potential and can be a great cryptocurrency in which to invest. Another currency worth investing in is Ethereum, as it is built on a specific type of blockchain that allows not only payments but also supports apps that provide a vast range of services from insurance policies to computer games. This type of technology is relatively new yet has enormous potential to grow.

How do you know the right cryptocurrency to invest in? Here are some tips.

> ➤ You need to analyze the cryptocurrency's attractiveness as an investment opportunity. You should look for steady growth over a period. Bitcoin, for example, could be a worthwhile investment based on this point.

> ➤ You should check the coin limit of the currency. Some cryptocurrencies have a certain number of coins that can be mined, and after that number is reached, no more will be produced. Bitcoin, for example, has a limit of 21 million coins. This is important as an unlimited number of coins can have a negative impact on the currency's value. On the other hand, a limited number of coins has the risk of deflation.

> ➤ If a coin has a large surrounding community and a lot of investors and participants, it indicated a possibility that the price will increase.

> ➤ Check what characteristics the coin has as this influences value. For example, Ether is required to use the Ethereum blockchain, so it has the potential for large-scale

use. Monero is another type of cryptocurrency. It provides total privacy for its users which is attractive for some people. This means its popularity will most likely continue.

➢ If the coin is a duplicate of an existing coin, it can be harder for it to find success on the market as it struggles to compete with its similar peer. However, some do have success as duplicates. Just look at Ethereum and Ethereum Classic or Bitcoin and Bitcoin Cash.

➢ If the coin is being marketed well, it has better potential to reach a larger audience. This is a good sign that it could be a worthy investment.

➢ Read as much news and white papers about the coin you are considering to invest in as possible. These authoritative documents will give you timely, accurate news about the performance of the coin, helping you to make better-informed decisions about which ones are doing well and which ones aren't.

Once you have decided to invest in a particular coin, you can buy some of the currency and start trading on the cryptocurrency exchanges. There are several different sites of cryptocurrency exchanges, and they each have their own set of characteristics that make them more attractive to some investors than others. Some work with a broader range of cryptocurrencies while others have lower fees than others. Check these details before using a particular exchange site.

Some of the most popular exchanges include Coinbase, Kraken, Shapeshift, and Bitstamp.

Here are some points worth considering when trading cryptocurrencies.

> ➢ You can either trade short-term or long-term. Short term is when you trade coins between a range of a few minutes to a couple of days. Long-term is when you buy coins and wait for months or even years for the value to go up and then selling. Short-term can be highly profitable but is best only for skilled and experienced investors. Long-term can still be very profitable, has less risk, and almost anyone can invest long-term.
>
> ➢ If you invest short-term, you must understand the exchange market well and be able to not only read trends but accurately predict what direction the value will take. This involves understanding the bigger picture and knowing how global events affect coin prices.
>
> ➢ Using a long-term trading strategy may not make you much money instantly, but it can be a plan.
>
> ➢ If you decide to do short-term trading, note that this often involves several transactions in one day to try and make a profitable outcome. However, it can be highly lucrative if you make the right decisions at precisely the right time.

Chapter Summary

In this chapter, we looked at how you can invest and trade cryptocurrency to make money.

- Cryptocurrency is a type of digital currency that is global, not restricted by exchange rates, operates on a decentralized network, and has anonymous accounts. The most popular and well-known cryptocurrency is Bitcoin. There are other currencies though that are also valuable such as Ethereum and Monero.

- Cryptocurrency can be highly profitable, primarily if you invest in the right one from the very beginning. For example, in 2010, one Bitcoin was valued at $0.08. Nowadays in 2017, one Bitcoin is valued at over $4,500.

- Choosing the right coin to invest in is important, and there are several considerations to consider before investing.

- You can sell your cryptocurrencies on specific exchanges online, such as Coinbase and Bitstamp.

- You can either trade your cryptocurrency short-term or long-term. Short-term can be highly profitable but also very risky. Long-term can still bring in good profits and has much lower risk.

In the next chapter, we will look at how you can make money through blogging.

Chapter Seven: How To Make Money Blogging

In this chapter, we will see how blogging can be a profitable source of income, and we'll see how some people manage to make blogging a full-time job.

Making money from a blog is becoming a trendy way of earning money as a freelancer. It is also surprisingly easy to do regarding opportunities available. Setting up a blog, maintaining it, generating traffic, and producing regular, top quality content takes a lot of time and effort. However, it will be your platform, and you will be your own boss which is immensely rewarding.

As you will be spending so much time on your blog, it is essential to write about something that you really have a passion about as that will convey in your work. However, a theme we have already touched upon is of niches. It is so important to make sure your blog serves a niche rather than a broad audience. This helps you to narrow your target audience and create content that is of real value for a compact segment rather than a lot of content to a vast audience that will only be vaguely interested in some of your articles. You want an engaged audience that follows your blog and will subscribe as they find the site fascinating and meets their particular needs.

What kind of niche are we talking here? Let's say you love to travel and you want to write a travel blog. The thing is, there are thousands of travel blogs out there, so you need to make yours different. What part of travel do you like? Are you interested in other things to or are there circumstances in your life that make you a minority type of traveler? For example, you could have a travel blog that explores vegan food around the world or a travel blog that looks at how to travel with disabilities. By defining clearly what you will be blogging about, it helps you to know your audience better and develop content that will suit them.

Making a blog is easy nowadays. You can use a website content management site such as WordPress to create your own website. Many of the themes are free to use and are easy to play around with to create a beautiful looking site. However, you want to use your blog to make money so it is best to have the most professional looking website you can afford. That's why it is better to pay for a web developer and designer to create the site for you including logo design and to make a site that reflects your brand. You need to have a strong brand that matches your niche so spend some time thinking about the voice of the brand and the colors that represent it. This should be clear throughout the entire site.

What are some of the best ways of monetizing your blog? Here are some ideas.

- Using per-click advertising. This is where you get paid for every click on an ad on your site. After you have signed up, the provider will give you a unique contextual ad that relates to the content you provide. For example, if you blog about free diving, you may have ads that show swimwear or mono-fins. There are several providers out there, but Google AdSense is one of the most popular. This is an excellent way of making a passive income, especially if your blog gets a lot of traffic.

- In text ads. These are ads placed inside articles. An in-text advertising provider will place a sponsored link inside the text that is double-underlined. If the user moves the cursor over the links, a pop-up appears with the product which the user can then click on if they are interested. You then gain money from the click on the ad.

- Advertising space. You can sell space on your site for ads. It is good to work only with companies that are in a similar field to you and whose ads will genuinely provide value for your readers. Many internet users are savvy when it comes to ads and find them off-putting, yet relevant ones tend to be received well. You can charge a lot for this if you have a site with high numbers of traffic.

- Product reviews. Companies can pay you to write a product review about one of their products. This is common among top bloggers who have many visitors per month. It is essential to only review products that relate to the topic of your blog. It would be strange and off-putting if you review a new makeup range if your blog is about local football teams.

- Writing an e-book and selling it through your blog is a great way of making an extra income. Your book should be an extension of the topics you write about on your blog and offer much more detail.

- Sell services. For example, if your blog is about pensions, you could offer your services through a 'hire me' type of format where people can pay for a consultation with you about the best pension plan for them.

Another prevalent way of making money on your blog is through affiliate marketing. This is something we will look at in the next chapter.

Chapter Summary

In this chapter, we looked at the different ways of making money on your blog.

- Making a blog nowadays is easy. There are plenty of great themes on WordPress that allows you to make your own blog for free and easily. However, if you want to make money from your blog, it's best to hire a professional web developer and designer who can do it for you. This will help your blog look better and stand out from the crowd.

- You should pick a subject that you feel passionate about for your blog. You should also aim to cater for a niche segment to help you focus on one topic in an area with less competition and a market that you will find it easier to understand and define.

- There are several ways of making money on your blog. For example, you can advertise, have pay-per-click advertising, do product reviews, or write sponsored posts.

In this next chapter, we will look at how you can make money on your blog using affiliate marketing.

Chapter Eight: Making Money Through Affiliate Marketing

In this chapter, we will look at ways you can make money through affiliate marketing.

First, let's begin by defining affiliate marketing. Affiliate marketing is when you promote someone else's products or services on your site, and you earn commission from the people that purchase the product through your site. For example, if you write an article about travel and you talk about where to find cheap flights. You can link the text to a flights comparison page that has an affiliate marketing programme that you have already signed up for. If someone clicks on the link in your article and buys a flight from that a page, you will earn a portion of that total sale.

To use affiliate marketing, you need to check the website has a programme and if it does, sign up for it. You will receive a special affiliate code that you put into your articles that trace back any sales from your site to you. This is how you earn money. You can also track your performance on the site's affiliate marketing page.

The three main types of affiliate marketing are:

➢ Pay per sale where you receive a commission for each sale you make through your blog.

➢ Pay per click where you receive a commission for every time a visitor clicks on an ad.

➢ Pay per lead where you earn commission from a number of leads you get from another company.

Which Affiliate Programmes Should You Use?

Several companies offer affiliate programmes. Check some companies within your niche and check their websites to see if they have information for affiliates. The two most universal and popular affiliate marketing programmes are Amazon and ClickBank.

Amazon is easy to set up, and it gives you thousands of items that you can link to from your site. For example, if you have a blog about camping, you can write articles about the essential equipment for a weekend camping in the rain. In your article, you can mention some of the best products that people would need and link these to Amazon. If a visitor clicks on the link and decides to purchase the product, you will make a commission from that sale. Amazon uses cookies on its affiliate programme.

What does this mean? It means that if someone clicks on a link from your site, you will still receive a commission even if that person buys the item within a 90-day period.

To use the Amazon affiliate programme, you need to sign up to it and fill out your business or blog details plus your bank details. Then you will receive your unique affiliate ID that will be connected to the links of the products you use from the Amazon site. It's worth noting that Amazon is strict with their affiliate programme and you must follow their rules and conditions. If not, you face losing your account. These rules include making sure you use a disclosure in each article that says you are using affiliate links in any articles where you do use them. Be sure to read through Amazon's terms and conditions to make sure you avoid any issues.

Another popular affiliate programme is ClickBank which has a similar concept to Amazon. It's free to use, and like Amazon, it has a vast range of items for sale. To use ClickBank, register for the affiliate programme and then find the product you want to promote on your blog. Copy your unique link that will be coded with your affiliate ID and add to your article. When visitors click on the link, they will be redirected to the product's sale page, and they will have the opportunity to purchase it.

There are other affiliate programmes you can use. Hotels.com is great for travel websites that talk about accommodation. You can add links to articles to specific hotels that you mention to earn a commission from every person that books a stay at the hotel. Other sites include GetYourGuide.com which has an affiliate programme for the hundreds of different excursions and activities they provide in dozens of cities across the world.

Here are some of the significant advantages of using affiliate marketing to monetize your blog.

> ➢ If you have a site that has a high volume of traffic, this is a great and simple way of earning a comfortable passive income stream.

> ➢ There are no fees at all for affiliate programmes. You simply need to sign up and add the links to your article. Then, if successful, you will start earning commission from the links.

> ➢ Your only concern needs to be creating engaging content that will bring a high volume of traffic. Issues such as customer support, shipping, and storage of the product are the concern of the company.

> ➢ Affiliate marketing reaches a global audience, so you have a potentially huge audience.

Chapter Summary

In this chapter, we looked at how you can use affiliate marketing to monetize your blog.

> - Affiliate marketing is when you promote a company's products or services on your site and if this turns into a conversion and the visitor pays a product, you

will earn a commission. You promote the product or service through a link added into a text where visitors can click on it and have the opportunity to buy the product.

- There are hundreds of affiliate programmes, and it pays to look around for what is available in your niche. However, the two most popular programmes are Amazon and ClickBank.

Using affiliate marketing is an excellent way of making a potentially highly profitable passive income stream, especially if your blog has high volumes of traffic.

Final Words

Thanks again for taking the time to download this book! I hope you enjoyed reading it and now feel inspired to start your own online business and create your own ways of making an income.

You should now have a good understanding of setting up an online business and how it's possible to create income from it. You should also be able to decide on the best service and product that you can offer to your potential clients and understand several ways of monetizing from your skillset and experience.

If you enjoyed this book, please take the time to leave me a review on Amazon. I appreciate your honest feedback, and it helps me to continue producing high-quality books.

About the author

31-year-old Anthony Parker is a self-made Internet entrepreneur, investor & author.

Anthony first entered the world of Online Business in 2014 with the creation of his first dropshipping store, since then Anthony has created and sold 3 other dropshipping stores and has since ventured out into Amazon FBA and Affiliate Marketing with the goal of creating long-term highly profitable passive income streams.

Anthony latest venture is to share his knowledge and passion on the world of Online Business with the goal of making seemingly complex and intimidating topics simple and easy-to-read with the hope of encouraging others to become internet entrepreneurs.

www.ingramcontent.com/pod-product-compliance
Lightning Source LLC
Chambersburg PA
CBHW071201240526
45470CB00017B/964